OFFICIALLY
WITHDRAWN

D1607237

MARS

BY NATH

BELLWETHER MEDIA ∘ MINNEAPOLIS, MN

TM

Are you ready to take it to the extreme? Torque books thrust you into the action-packed world of sports, vehicles, mystery, and adventure. These books may include dirt, smoke, fire, and chilling tales. **WARNING**: read at your own risk.

This edition first published in 2019 by Bellwether Media, Inc.

Library of Congress Cataloging-in-Publication Data

Names: Sommer, Nathan, author.
Title: Mars / by Nathan Sommer.
Description: Minneapolis, MN : Bellwether Media, Inc., [2019] | Series: Torque. Space Science | Audience: Ages 7-12. | Audience: Grades 3 to 7. | Includes bibliographical references and index.
Identifiers: LCCN 2018039178 (print) | LCCN 2018039616 (ebook) | ISBN 9781681036915 (ebook) | ISBN 9781626179738 (hardcover : alk. paper)
Subjects: LCSH: Mars (Planet)—Juvenile literature.
Classification: LCC QB641 (ebook) | LCC QB641 .S66 2019 (print) | DDC 523.43—dc23
LC record available at https://lccn.loc.gov/2018039178

Editor: Kate Moening   Designer: Andrea Schneider

Printed in the United States of America, North Mankato, MN.

TABLE OF CONTENTS

MARS'S SALTY SEA

It is March 23, 2004. **NASA** scientists look on in wonder as they study images from the Mars **rover** *Opportunity*. The photos show the rocky coast of a once salty sea.

Opportunity shows that Mars once had more water than Earth's Arctic Ocean. If this Earth-like planet had gigantic bodies of water, did it support life, too?

ILLUSTRATION OF *OPPORTUNITY* ROVER

WHAT IS MARS?

Mars is one of the smallest planets in the solar system. It is only larger than Mercury. At 4,222 miles (6,795 kilometers) across, it is about half the size of Earth.

Mars is nicknamed the "Red Planet" for the red dust that covers much of its surface. Its **atmosphere** is very thin and made mostly of the gas carbon dioxide.

MARS VS. EARTH
SIZE COMPARISON

HEAT WAVE

Mars is not always a frozen desert! It heats up to
86 degrees Fahrenheit (30 degrees Celsius) during
its warmest months.

Mars shares much in common with Earth.
The Red Planet has many **canyons**, valleys,
and **volcanoes**. Mars's total land area is about
the same as Earth's.

HOW FAR AWAY IS MARS?

MARS TO EARTH = 49,000,000 MILES (78,900,000 KILOMETERS)

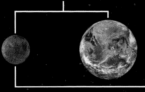

MARS TO SUN = 142,000,000 MILES (228,000,000 KILOMETERS)

This dry, frozen planet is windy and foggy. Like Earth, its days are about 24 hours long. Mars also has changing seasons. But its thin atmosphere makes it much colder than Earth.

HOW DID MARS FORM?

Mars formed around 4.6 billion years ago. The solar system was just a giant dust cloud then. **Gravity** pulled the dust into different clumps. These clumps eventually became planets!

Scientists think **asteroids** hitting the planet's surface brought water with them. Mars was covered in lakes, rivers, and a huge ocean. Most of this water froze or became gas over time.

ILLUSTRATION OF
MARS WITH WATER

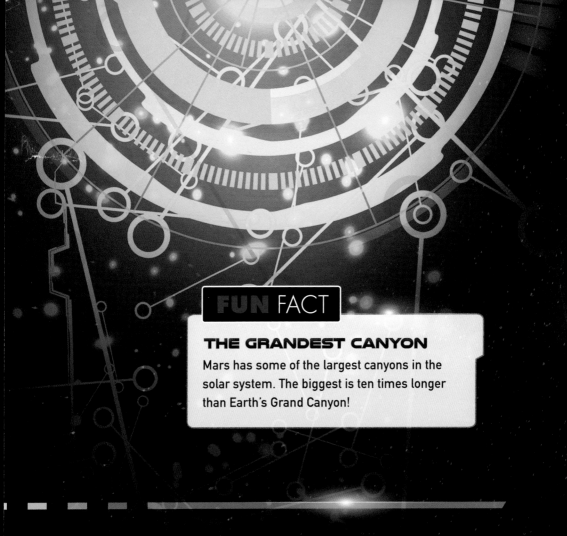

THE GRANDEST CANYON

Mars has some of the largest canyons in the solar system. The biggest is ten times longer than Earth's Grand Canyon!

Mars has cooled to mostly frozen temperatures today. The northern half is a flat desert covered in sand.

Mars's southern half is filled with **craters**. Valleys there show that a large channel of rivers once flowed through the area. The center of the planet has many volcanoes.

MARS VS. EARTH

OLYMPUS MONS
16 MILES (26 KILOMETERS)

MOUNT EVEREST
5.5 MILES (8.9 KILOMETERS)

VALLES MARINERIS
2,500 MILES (4,023 KILOMETERS)

GRAND CANYON
277 MILES (446 KILOMETERS)

Both **poles** of Mars have ice caps made of frozen carbon dioxide. The caps grow during the coldest seasons. They get smaller in warmer weather.

Mars has powerful dust storms during warmer seasons. They are so strong and huge that they actually change the way Mars's surface looks.

CARBON DIOXIDE ICE CAP
ON MARS'S NORTH POLE

WHERE IS MARS FOUND?

Mars is the fourth planet from the Sun. It sits between Earth and the **asteroid belt**. Only Venus gets closer to Earth than Mars.

Two small moons, Phobos and Deimos, **orbit** Mars. The planet itself orbits the Sun once every 687 days. Its years are almost twice as long as Earth's years!

FUN FACT

DUAL MOONS

In ancient Greek stories, the god Ares had two sons. Their names were Phobos and Deimos. Mars's moons are named for them! Phobos means "fear" and Deimos means "panic."

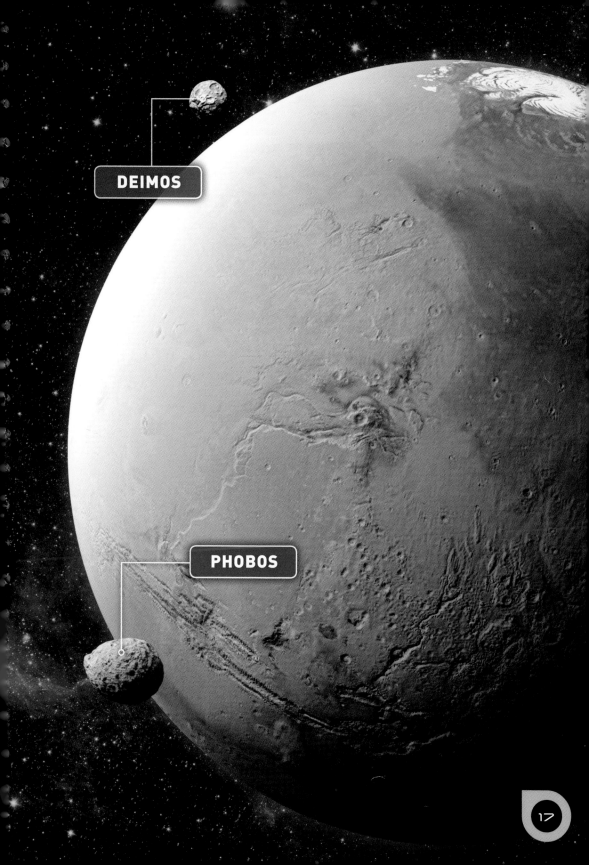

DEIMOS

PHOBOS

WHY DO WE STUDY MARS?

Scientists study Mars because it is so Earth-like. It once had water. Does this mean it also had life? Rovers such as *Opportunity* search its surface for any signs.

Mars and Earth probably looked alike when they formed. But Earth's surface went through changes that Mars's did not. Rocks on Mars look like they did millions of years ago! Studying them helps scientists figure out Earth's history.

CURIOSITY ROVER

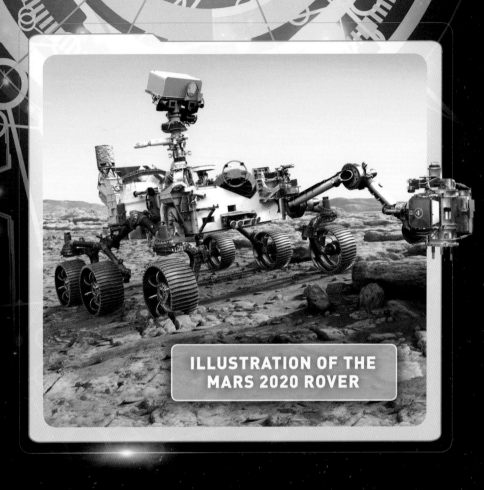

ILLUSTRATION OF THE
MARS 2020 ROVER

NASA plans to send humans to Mars by the 2030s. **Astronauts** are training for life far from Earth. But a lot of hard, expensive work must be done before then.

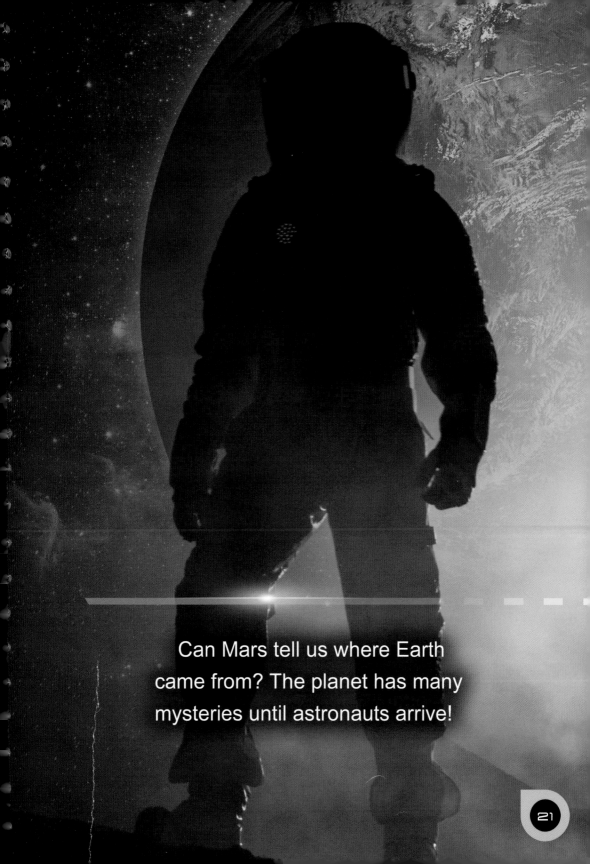

Can Mars tell us where Earth came from? The planet has many mysteries until astronauts arrive!

GLOSSARY

asteroid belt–a part of space between Mars and Jupiter where many asteroids orbit the Sun

asteroids–small rocky objects that orbit the Sun

astronauts–scientists who explore and study space

atmosphere–the gases that surround Mars and other planets

canyons–deep, rocky valleys

craters–deep holes in the surface of an object

gravity–the force that pulls objects toward one another

NASA–National Aeronautics and Space Administration; NASA is a U.S. government agency responsible for space travel and exploration.

orbit–to move around something in a fixed path

poles–either end of a planet or star; every planet or star has two poles.

rover–a small vehicle sent to Mars by NASA to take pictures and study the planet's soil

volcanoes–vents that let out hot rocks and steam

TO LEARN MORE

AT THE LIBRARY

DeYoe, Aaron. *Space Travel.* Minneapolis, Minn.: Super Sandcastle, 2016.

Morey, Allan. *Mars Rovers.* Minneapolis, Minn.: Bellwether Media, 2018.

Payment, Simone. *Mars.* New York, N.Y.: Britannica Educational Publishing, 2017.

ON THE WEB

FACTSURFER

Factsurfer.com gives you a safe, fun way to find more information.

1. Go to www.factsurfer.com.

2. Enter "Mars" into the search box.

3. Click the "Surf" button and select your book cover to see a list of related web sites.

INDEX

The images in this book are reproduced through the courtesy of: Nerthuz, front cover, pp. 2, 7; NASA/JPL/ Cornell University/ NASA Images, pp. 4-5, 8-9; NASA/ NASA Images, pp. 6-7, 10-11, 21 (Earth); Jurik Peter, pp. 12-13; Vadim Sadovski, pp. 14-15; Dotted Yeti, pp. 16-17; NASA/JPL-Caltech/Malin Space Science Systems/ NASA Images, p. 19; NASA/JPL-Caltech/ NASA Images, p. 20; Gorodenkoff, pp. 20-21 (astronaut).